BLACK ROSE

BLACK ROSE

Sheefah Zarma

Copyright ©2018 SHEEFAH ZARMA

ISBN: 978-978-965-580-9

All rights reserved.
No part of this book may be reproduced, distributed, stored in a retrieval system, or transmitted, in any form or by any means, electronic, electrostatic, magnetic tape, mechanical, photocopying, recording, or otherwise without prior written permission from the Publisher.
For information about permission to reproduce selections from this book, write to info@wrr.ng

National Library of Nigeria Cataloguing-in-Publication Data

Cover Design: Akila Jibrin

Printed and Published in Nigeria by:
Words Rhymes & Rhythm Limited
Suite C309, Global Plaza Plot 366, Obafemi Awolowo Way, Jabi District, Abuja, Nigeria.
08169027757, 08060109295
www.wrr.ng

ACKNOWLEDGEMENT

This book wouldn't come to light, without the intellectual support of my family, especially my parents for the financial and mental support you rendered. I am glad I'm blessed with relatives like you.

I also want to thank my amazing friend, Abdulbaseet, thanks for being there for me
intellectually and believing in me.

This book wouldn't be complete without the amazing illustrations of Loui Jover and Pietro Tenuta

I am grateful.

CONTENTS

ACKNOWLEDGEMENT V

PETALS.. 2

THORNS 18

LEAVES 57

STEM 77

ROOTS 106

"I am a woman in process. I'm just trying like everybody else. I try to take every conflict, every experience, and learn from it. Life is never dull."

— **Oprah Winfrey**

"This will be my revenge: that one day you'll hold in your hands the book of a famous poet and you'll read these lines that the author wrote for you and you won't even know it"

— **Ernesto Cardenal**

PETALS

I wish you came a bit earlier
I wish we discovered this impeccable rapport earlier
Why did we stare from far away for too long?
These mountains between us are quickly devouring our happiness
Why did we take half step at a time
If I were to voice out the *whys*
It would take me forever
But the only answer is changeless
Therefore, fate cannot be cheated
You were just here to give me some momentary happiness.

O mine
A glass of wine wouldn't hurt
To wind up our hearts to twine
In every corner of our minds.

You make my heart smile so hard
That someone stealing a glance
Would think pain never visited me.

I like how your presence
Resurrects the naughty angels in me
I crave your lips for dessert.

One beautiful Monday night
Seventeen pink roses were banded beautifully
With a black luminous band

Beautifully seated as a beautiful bouquet
She couldn't stop smiling
After sighting such sweet surprise
From none other than her sweet sugarplum.

I love you
I want us to make it to heaven together
You see
I am not holding your body alone
My spirit and soul are holding yours as well
I want you to feel my love
And feel my pain
Hold me when the sunlight fades away
Lean on me when your life gets cloudy

You see
I *gotcha* like
Bonny got *Clyde*
I *gotcha*

We won't be outlaws
We would be mullahs
You and I against the transgressors.

I crave a love
Where the man of my dreams would evanesce
Ignite sparks of passion from his stares
Douse the flames of uncertainty from my heart
Hold my neck with mild touches, like hands to a kitten
And I would feel his lips
As sweet as honey and smooth as milk
And unquenchable like water to the desert.

You and I
Both know
This love of ours is poison
But we rather take the gamble

What's true love?
Without the sprinkle of tragedy.

Your voice makes me dwell in the abyss of bewilderment,
Just as it disarms my intelligence quotient.

Dear future husband
Know that I'm not an incurable romantic
But I'm playful
I'm not too secluded and clouded in being all clingy-cute
I'm a teaser. I'm the kind of wife
Who will need a friend in her husband
More than a lover

You said I was a lady of few words
But I wanted you to read the unspoken words in my eyes

Don't they say more than enough?

There are days I would give up the arms of my
lover and run to yours
Choose yours
Wrap my arms around yours
Place my head on your shoulder
And my actions will tell you how I missed you
Your heart knows our friendship is never
replaceable
Because that grey *gay-less* area is where we
belong.

Our lips wouldn't twine
Our hearts wouldn't bind
Our souls wouldn't mind
If his heart never bloomed like mine.

Sometimes, all you need to ignite your luminous shine
Is an unconditional love
From a person who gives unrequited love to others.

Being unperturbed by slanders led us here
We will always wear these badges of scars
As a sign of our strength
They ought to know we are non-quitters
We are here to make forever.

Dear future husband
Don't just put a ring on it
I want days you'll hold my hands
So gentle, like fragile glass
And kiss it passionately
Like a mothers love to her child
I want that kind of uncommon gallantry

I won't keep these stares to myself
Till your hands tune to the rhythm of my eyes

Kiss me in the rain
Let me feel the rhythm of the night tickle in my toes
Let me feel that breathless rush of adrenaline in my veins
O! mute out and tame those chaotic, circumambient noises
Give me that classic love
I so much crave.

There are days I would trade those boring meetings
I would trade that romantic movie with bae
I would even trade that mint lemonade
To be with you
Because you always remind me of how my stomach could ache
From mirthful, unimaginable laughter.

I'll be your dose of tranquillity in chaos
I'll embolden your spirits in doubt
I'll remind you that you're a pearl on days you feel valueless
I'll be your stamina whenever you are frail
I'll be your luminous conscience in darkness
I'll be your redemption if you ever stray
I will never give up on you
Because we are inter-twined, *Honey*

They tried to stunt our growth
Placing our minds in a jar
But they forgot we are beautiful seeds
So we grew in love
And blossomed like the flowers we were.

If giving you this heart
Signifies my love for you?
Then I would cut open my chest
To hand it over to you a million times more
.

I like how our souls are interwoven
Like a beautiful cardigan
I like how our bodies are twirled together
Like threads circled in bondage
My heart smiles
Knowing our destinies align in merriment
I love how destiny chose you for me
And I, for you
Some might see this bondage as pain
But only we who can feel it
Understand its beauty.

Come to me
All bare
From your masculinity
No, don't take off your shoes
Show me your badge of scars
Tell me your fears
Show me your vulnerability and insecurity
Drape off that robe of silence

Come to me
All bare
Uncage your demons
Show me your black feathers

Come to me all bare
I will never judge you
I will never belittle you
Let me see your ugliness
Let me embrace your imperfections
Every man deserves unconditional love
I will love you same
If not more

Just like a bulb to electricity
Your touches torch my soul
and ignites sparks of love.

Let me be the one you call
Whenever you need a listening ear
Let me be the one you call
Whenever you need a shoulder to cry on
Let me be the one you call
Whenever you need a confidant

Let me be your muse
Let me be the pulse in your soul
Let me be your sun, moon and the stars
Let me be your silver lining

Let me be your shadow
Whenever you feel alone
Let me be your luminous fairy
Whenever your path is gloomy
Let me be your kaleidoscope of lovely flowers
Whenever your life is colorless

Let our souls intertwine
Let's reproduce with love
Let's nurture our reproduced flowers
Let's grow old together
Dear future husband

I closed my eyes to sleep
And I found myself in the abyss of dreamland
I can't particularly conjure the mental picture in my head
But he left a note in his eyes

His eyes betrayed volumes of unspoken adventures
Eyes that cures acrophobia
Making you want to dive into the abyss of his soul

His smile felt like a beautiful diamond shining through an embedded rock
His beard is full, with shiny silky hairs
That sleep beautifully on his skin
And his voice
So charming, so captivating
It makes you wonder if he's truly human
Or just a figment of my imagination
But no, I wasn't dreaming
He's real

He asked for my heart with a big smile
But I managed to smile back
Holding it sternly with both hands
He noticed the sudden hard grip
And asked again
But my eyes were already battling back a puddle of tears
He moved closer and held my slippery heart
But I stole it back
As tears cascade down my cheeks
He uttered these words
'This is mine to please, heal and mend
Please don't deny me my right'

I don't need to tell you how your touch feels
My breath says more than any words could.

Come on honey
Don't just watch me bite these tasteless fingers of mine
Give me some of your sugar.

THORNS

Sometimes,
The only place I find solace
Is in the arms of pain
Realm of ghosts
Plate of thorns
Duvet of nightmares
And house of imaginary suicide.

You use to be the sun
Which lit my life brightly
And the sugar which made my life sweet
But now you are the sun that only burns my skin
And the diabetes that devours my soul.

Just tell me what you want now
By wrapping around my soul
Tell me what you need now
When all my life
I've been chasing you
But you kept disappointing me.

You physically bruised me
Emotionally broke me into shards
Mentally exhausted my sanity
And tossed my self-esteem
Into a bottomless sea
As I sank to the ground
Feeling manacled to my numb feet.

Last night
A scene from our written memories flashed
Looking at your face wasn't the problem
Locking eyes with you was the problem
I tried to blank stare without succeeding
Until some hoodlums passed by
And your insecure nature flashed
I didn't realize my laughter
Until I felt the grasping pain in my stomach
Nostalgia was an unfair friend
It wilted my walls of strength
To a bare skin of vulnerability
In few seconds
He saw what I was trying to hide
And our eyes could not lie
I miss us, and it hurts.

Underneath my smile
Lies a concealed world of pain
Bottled up in the jar of strength
With every pain puncturing its walls
And every agony scraping its surface
Still, a smile holds up the balance of my circumambient
But this time around
A sharp pain pierced the walls of my jar

And I can no longer hold down the pain
And my heart shatters into shards.

Bla! Bla! Bla!
I've heard this word
Way too many times
From takers of hearts
And givers of empty promises.

I cover up
To avoid attracting the wrong people
They still extra zoom through my cape

He tells me I'm beautiful
But his eyes are cheerfully affixed
To my bosom as he says so

I turn him away
But he defends himself shamelessly
With phrases like
'but did I say anything offensive?'

He forgets one could say more with body language.

My heart cracked
My eyes bled
To be the wine
To put to sleep my awoken pains.

Don't ask me
To tell you what resides in my heart
Because for me to house you there
Ought to be rhetoric
To feel my warmth
Feel my vibe
Feel my love
But you couldn't
Because yours is unrequited.

Wear this robe of guilt
It's enough to kiss you all night
In disconsolation.

You used my silence against me
But I still remained silent
You shot your vile words at me
I still showed benevolence to your spite
You shot at me again with your piercing arrows
I still stayed mute
You laughed at my silence and called me a coward
But I was only silent for you to see what eyes could not
You managed to bring me down
But I'll rise again
Because a humane heart never fails a test
My humanity will speak to the wise
I just hope you're among the wise.

Our feelings have diluted from red to yellow
And it hurts so badly.

We all have our off days
Days we don't care about being courteous
We don't have the stomach to hold in pains
Days we look for the amiable spirit in us
But it's nowhere to be found
Days we don't care about grooming our words
before voicing them
Days we are married to desolation
And we are comfortable with that wedlock
You shouldn't feel bad you have those days
Everyone has them too.

Make my heart bleed through my eyes
And I'll make sure your heart burns
Through my flamed hands.

Her father is a modest earner
At least he tries to feed them
Put a modest roof above their heads
And modest clothes on their body
But she is ungrateful
She'd rather sell a commodity
That stays with the seller
Her body.

Her parents eat twice
To keep up with the trend
She eats at five star hotels and drives a car
While her parents take the bus
She flaunts money of various currencies on the media
But she is neither a civil servant nor a business tycoon

Well, clap for yourself
We all understand where it comes from
It's a token of the pleasure
Being sought in-between your thighs.

Some say
I refuse to get married
Because I am waiting for a prince charming
Another says no
She isn't interested in royalty
She is waiting for a fair handsome man
Another says no
She doesn't fancy superficial beauty
Perhaps she is waiting for a billionaire
Can't you see her father isn't poor?
While another says no
She isn't materialistic
But an old woman seated in their midst says
She is waiting for none other than time.

In every poet exists
A puddle of bleeding hearts and eyes
Sleeping underneath the ocean of sensitivity.

But you told me to stay away from him
He is only after my body
I thought you cared
So I ran to you as a confidant
Never did I know you were studying my weakness
Which you prepared and used against me
But then again
Such is life.

Don't tell a lady with lamentation in her heart that she's too broken for you
Don't tell a lady who made a barrier with her past, that she's questionably too good for you,
Don't stomp on someone's self-esteem and tell them they aren't worthy of the respect they earned
Just don't bring negativity into someone's life and expect to be
tolerated for eternity.

Sometimes I sit to think
On why she chose to demean her family's' name
Choosing to jump from one mans' bed another
Repeatedly saving that money

But the money is unconsciously seeping through her hands
It's like fetching water from a well
With a leaking bucket
It will always be full
But before it gets to you
The water in the bucket has long seeped out
Why don't you see how you've made yourself a prisoner to wealth?

My heart was the plaintiff
And I the defendant
It filed a lawsuit against me
For constant emotional trauma

In my defence
I pointed the case as a mistrial
I noted an ignored liquidated claim
Giving my reasons...

'we are intertwined, it's better to be
emotionally sensitive than to
be sadistic or uncharitable

you are a heart, you were created to
sustain life, give love and feel love, not
spread spite and spill
hate'
As the case was remand to the jury
And I was pleaded 'not guilty'.

How can I give you my heart?
When you have another in yours
Tell me where you plan to keep mine
Don't dare think
I'll settle in a detached extension
My heart cannot share
You give me all of you or none of you
This heart will only settle
When your heart has no tenant.

You said unrequited love was not yours to take
I never believed you
When you left
I never marinated the meaning in between your lines
Till you left me alone with my heart
Unable to console me
I don't know which was worse
To be left with my heart to keep
Or to give my heart to be toyed with?

My heart has turned blue
With the gruelling echo of your absence
Each day turning to a crescendo of misery
I will soon drown in this pool of tears
With tides of unspoken sea ghosts
I didn't realize I was visually impaired
Until I couldn't sight the bucket you kicked right in front of me
Why did you leave me so soon?
When death heard us toast to forever.

You came to my door
You said you were here to stay

You told my ears what they craved to hear
Spoke to my heart the way it yearned to be spoken to
Healed my soul with warming stunts
At some point I swore to my conscience
We were making forever
But the moment I said I loved you
Was the moment your eyes ignited
With a spark of something only I could read
But eyes don't lie you see
While your sweet lips, heart and soul lied to my unlocking face.

Why would you tell me
Stories of Nelson Mandela
And how you wished more were like him
But when I said I wanted to be like him
You told me to simply mind my business
If I don't plan for an untimely death
Leaving me in a focused confusion
Still trying to juggle the genuineness in your wish.

I would rather walk away from this insanity
I call love
Than to stay and lack an iota of sanity.

There are days
I allow the ghosts touch me
Because I'm tired of being touched by people full of this life
When they prove to me
They are full of ghosts
And that beating heart is just a drum.

You meant your words
When you said you'd never give up on us
Fighters don't quit

You meant your words
When you said you'd kill for me
I should have known you were a psychopath
Love made my hearing impaired

You meant your words
When you pierced my heart
With your sharp spear of lies

You meant your words
When you shot down the Cupid in me

If only I tasted your sugar coated lies
I could have known its poison
If only I paid attention to the semantics in your words
And not the phonetics
I could have emotionally survived.

You sought an escape from a bottle
When the bottle itself cages souls
This liquor will only set your pains in equilibrium
And remodel your problems
When reality starts to seep back into your soul
And later to your head.

I can still feel the scorching scars
You jabbed and engraved on my skin
I can still feel the devouring pain
Eating up my mind
I am emotionally famished.

I recall the days
When all we had was each other
But, sadly, our feelings are declining
And flying away like birds in the skies.

You haven't walked in my shoes
You haven't walked in my path
You haven't shed the tears my eyes did
You haven't been wilted time and again
You haven't been once helplessly held down
You haven't been abused in your childhood
You haven't been pricked by thorns
You haven't felt death while still alive
You haven't been misconstrued time and again
No you haven't been me for a single second
To know what I went through
Don't you dare try to tell me
I don't know what pain is.

This obsessive feeling has clogged my brain
Pinned the wings of my heart
Doused the flames of my courage
Ignited the sparks of my cowardice
Marinated my soul in doubt
As tears cascade down my cheeks
Like water running down a hill
As I watch my crush

Walk to another woman.

There are moments
I feel my strength seeping out of my body
Like sand in an hourglass
The light in my soul dims low
Like a tuned down chandelier
The strength in my voice breaks
Like shattered glass being walked upon
And my body so frail and cold
Like a lifeless corpse
With my eyes red soaked in tears
Like a red towel sprayed out to dry
And in that moment
The only thing I need
Is a shoulder to cry on.

I can't tell you what hatred is
Neither can I explain it
But I can tell you a bit about pity
And a lot about karma.

How could you ask me to trust you?
When words are cheap
How could you tell me you're different?
And you seek only my hand and not my body
I asked you to prove yourself
But the first thing you did was grab my bosoms
Only then did I truly believe you are different
But despicably different.

Love comes with an unimaginable force
It disarms you completely
It shatters your egotistic wall
Breaking you into shards of vulnerability
O love
Such genuine beauty you possess
Yet destructive force it yields
If impersonated.

I never knew this love was homicide
I thought this love would revive the beat in my heart

Never did I knew
You were here to silence it.

She displays her debauchery to the world
Like dishes on a platter
She's neither self-employed nor a civil servant
She doesn't catch feelings
She only catches flights
Obsessed she is with the media
Never would she cover *'The meeting scene'*
But you will always see the outcome of such encounters
Money flaunted like a badge of honor
When it's obviously a symbol of dishonor
A post to fuel her conceited self
Having her ask a rhetorical question
On why she's still single
But, *Dear Sister*
Isn't that enough a reason?

Sometimes all I need is a hard grip
That holds my soul
And not these empty, heavy promises.

Many have journeyed through this soul
But no one has ever doused
The flames of my pains.

I rather hug this cactus
At least they show their true nature
Unlike the way your roses hide their thorns.

You were the only sister I accepted
The only I called a home
And you chose to be a cannibal
Having me as your daily meal
I was just wilting
Day after day

I came to you wailing
Saying I feel eaten
You always embraced me in sheets of deceit

I got over your betrayal
And left the strange heart I called a home
Now you're knocking on my door?
I'm sorry I can't let you into my home again.

When we met
Your lips spoke to me
As your soul did
Your voice spoke lies
As your eyes transcribed the truth
I want your eyes to speak to me
When your lips are shut
And I want your heart to speak to me
When your voice is voiceless.

I don't even fear ghosts anymore
All they do with their frightening look is stare
What scares me to my spine is
A handsome man with venomous lips.

She heard too many empty promises
This weighed her heart
And altered its purpose
Her heart still throbs
Solely for the sake of survival
She was pushed into believing
Love only exists fictionally
You can tell she's despondent from love
Empty heavy promises made her dispirited
Falling had a different meaning
To her ,it's just getting hurt
The only love she knew was unrequited love
Given time and again
To takers who only took love as a word
She became unsentimental
But you will always see her drowning in a sea of schmaltz
You might think she's a dreamer
But she's a realist
Apparently an incurious being towards love
She writes beautifully about it
But you'd be astounded to realize
She's far from a realistic, incurable, romantic
She is me.

It's tough to decide on whether to give up or hold unto him
But this heart, mind, soul and brain are deceptive,
And all I'm left with
Is a friend called confusion
And it's brightly smiling back at me
With a vile, sarcastic smile.

I simply have no words for you
I'll allow your guilt to eat you up
With hope that nothing is left of you
And karma serves you what you deserve.

You told me you wouldn't walk away
When I opened my doors to you
I told you others have broken this heart like glass
You said all you saw was light that shone
Like sunrays behind an envious cloud

You said you would be my home
And I shall not worry
You told me I would be flawless
If I rid away the past hurt
And I mended all my broken pieces
You said you adored me for that
But you scanned through and saw no iota of pain
Only for you to knock me down like a bulldozer to a wall

As my pieces crumbled and fell
You flee like the hawks I said I met
But, why?

This empty vessel yearns for a painter
All you could hear are hoots of owls
Flocking around my caged, blue soul
When you should hear the songs from a nightingale
Hailing and rising with a good spirit of love
Please paint out the blue
And paint it yellow
Red is overrated
Yellow is more genuine.

Sometimes I wish I never had a pure heart
Like, be mean, blunt and unfazed about it
Hurt people and be nonchalant about it
Be standoffish and be cool about it
Discommodate people and be comfortable about it
But writing all of these sad wishes
Make me feel bad already.

This heart of yours only burns like a furnace
Can't you see how my body thaws from your scorching flames?
This love burns, it doesn't heal
Let me flee before you devour my sanity too.

Yes, your lips uttered love
But your eyes uttered lust.

He could be the freest
As a flying eagle
Be the prideful
As a royal horse
Be the perpetually ill-tempered
As a bull
Be as fiercely built as *King Kong*
But a faceless thigh
Could disarm him in seconds
Can't you see?
He's a happy slave.

There are days when my petals turn colorless
When the fire in my soul flakes away
When the lioness in me purrs
When the leaves on me wilt and crumble down
When the bones in my body feel numb
When my roses turns to cactus
When my feathers feels pinned and clipped
When my fears unchain themselves
As this colorless, *terrorful* feeling consumes me
Causing me to drown slowly

The only remedy I needed
Was to be told things
I'd like to tell a loved one
On a colorless day.

You loved me unconditionally
Only concerned with who I was with him
His fiancée
Wedlock was something I admired
Staying married is something I fantasized
Starting my family was my little dream

As I woke up
One unpromising day
I didn't know what changed
But all I could say now is I wasn't myself then
When I said I couldn't tie the knots with you
I needed help and no one saw it
You saw me slipping away
All you did was cry
When all you could have done was pray

Now I'm healing
All I want is to knot the tie with you
But I'm still afraid of myself
If I'll bail out on you one more time
And this time around
I wouldn't forgive me
Because neither you nor myself know
Where this feeling is coming from.

My mind wanders with questions
My mind uses words and phrases my mouth can't
dare utter
My mind is fearless
My mind speaks unstoppable, mighty things in
your presence
My heart tells it to shut up
My heart tells it not to utter things that may
cause harm

If only my mind is voiced
It could have put me in trouble for voicing out
the voiceless things it says
But voiceless thoughts are like poison drops
across my soul
It kills me inside slowly
And it kills me more outside
Because I dare not use my voiced mouth to utter
the length, might and
measurable dangers my mind utters

I sit back like a retard
I smile like a profound disable
And with a weak my voice say:
'I'm fine.'

I'm in a melancholic world
Few could notice
My soul feels manacled
I still manage a smile
I swear, I am cheerful
When consumed
Instantly sullen; I become
Sometimes abashedly inhibited
To evade being withdrawn
But then again
Fate whispered
'Remember the silver lining'
As I smile in my hopeless-FULL state of comatose.

Just when you think he's different
And distinct from the rest
He proves you wrong
And acts like the rest
They are all after one thing
He loves you from the bottom of his bottom.

The slanderer chose you
Because he knows you are the simpleton who
believes without proof.

LEAVES

This heart is not of flesh only
But of soil to grow
Of seeds to reproduce goodness
Of flowers to add color to others
To be a home and shelter for the needy

This heart is a giver
This heart is never a quitter
It will never give up on humanity.

You may hurt me
You may crumble my petals
You may forcefully open my buds
You may betray me
You may shatter my walls
But the least I could; is cry it out
And pray for you to be a changed person
And the worst I could do to you
Is pray you feel what you made me feel.

Give me thorns
I'll always give you my petals
Because I will forever be colorful
And you will forever be brown
That is enough a curse.

These eyes were trained
To see the beauty in people
And that includes the beauty in my foes.

As long as blood still flows in my veins
Air still pumps in my lungs
Heart still beats in my chest
I will always be forever green
My leaves will never dry out
My leaves will never fall off
You may wilt my leaves
But they will spring back up
They will rejuvenate
Because this heart is full of humanity
And yours is full of malice.

Do not look down
On the person who looks down to talk to you
Do not raise your voice
At the person who lowered his voice to speak to you
Do not use your power over a person
Who is powerless over you
It is not because you are wiser
Or you deserved the mercies that came your way
It is simply because God chose to favor you
And He wants to see how you use your blessings on others
How you treat others
Says how rich you are at heart.

You said I was too good to be true
Holding a smirk on your face
'Show me the skeleton in your cupboard!'
You roared
As I humbly pulled off my skin
So you see the skeleton in me
But you were mute in bewilderment
To see my skeleton blossom and shine with brightness
Like a garden in heaven.

You don't need someone who would preach love
to you
You need someone who could practice kindness
to you

Love is overrated
Kindness is rare.

The worst kind of poverty
Is to be a pauper in humanity.

I do not have any designer shoes or bags
My clothes are from random, normal stores
I do not apply any SPF when going out
I do not have body hydrants nor face primers
I do not live in a mansion
Neither are my meals a balanced diet I can't afford

I do not have a car or a bicycle
Neither do I have designer perfumes
Yet, I'm still happy

I know you think I'm foolish
With that sarcastic look of yours
But honestly, I wonder
Who lied to you that happiness is based on the material?
When it's all about being with God

He gave me health, happiness and contentment
And a family that cares
I couldn't ask for more.

The generous man
Is neither foolish
Nor unaware of the value of his money

The miserly thinks
The more he is selfish
The longer his wealth sustains

But a lettered man in his worship knows
The more he gives
The more God sends his way.

If you are okay with the natural phenomenon of
having asymmetrical fingers
Then you should be okay with the fact that
Someone will always be more than you
As well as yourself being more than another
It's nature's natural way of revolution.

It took a VOICE to make history
It took a DECISION to practice change
It took COURAGE to stand alone
It took FATE to stay determined
It took DESTINY to unfold its suspense
It took FAITH to keep you away from doubt.

And now
It took ME years to realize a decision is all I need to take in order
to make my voice shine through, with courage as I believe my faith
won't let me down nor will my destiny change.
But it has everything
to do with my fate.

When the weight of the world came crumbling on me
And the mountains I carried consumed me
Having the only place I found solace was with the cactus
But a mocking bird came to sing
Not an owl or a hawk
Only then did I see clearly
How my daunting pain was all in my head.
I'm innocent!

I saw how thirsty you are
Sitting with your crown of thorns
I know you are beautiful from a distance
But untouchable
Despite your nature
I came to water you
But you still pricked me with your thorns
It hurt inside more than it did outside
But I got over it
Knowing I'll still be your giver
Even if you hurt me

You should know a sunflower never grows thorns.

Some people call me foolish
      Naïve
           Dumb
For treating my foes with kindness
But what I want them to remember is
They are crooked
And I am not
So how can a person who knows no malice
Be wicked.

You want endless mirth?
Go for a joker
He is an impeccable lover
But be ready to have your feelings joked with.

My eyes rains
My heart floods
My mind hurricanes at his sight
He lost faith in the government
He rather dreams a better life
He doesn't wish to waste a tear
Neither does he want to waste a word
So he keeps mute
But her darling
Cheer up!
A greener life lies ahead
Vibrantly greener than the trees in your compound
You will soar high and touch that silver linen.

Fate doesn't have a manmade cure
Its only cure is time.

Tsk! Tsk! Tsk!
Too bad!
Mirrors only capture superficial appearances
And too bad for the men
Who follow her for her looks
It only gets easier to shackle a bait.

Let them beg you
With phrases of praises
Hiding under the curtain of ridicule
Grace their empty, stretched hands
With what they wish to receive
Give not because you are a simpleton
Give because you do it for the Most High
And that has nothing to do with
How hypocritical they are.

I always conceal my secrets
And enshroud my hidden skeletons
But if I rip my heart open
And show you my anatomy
Only then will you know
You are not just a friend but a confidant
As you are expected to confidently cloak my diaries.

So what you drive the most expensive cars
So what you own the jets
So what you wear the best
So what you eat the best
So what you live in a mansion
So what!
If you don't respect people
You are worthless in the eyes of humanity.

You call me poor
But I'm richer than you at heart
You laughed sarcastically and called me a fool
But I smiled back and said
'By God I am wise'
You sneered in contempt
But I stared in happiness
You nodded in disbelief
I nodded in confidence
You felt I was a long shot from exposure
I felt you were a long shot from gratitude
You felt I was mentally blind
And I felt you were faithfully blind
'Let's cut the story short'
I uttered
Just go with your love for the worldly
Allow me to continue my happy trial in peace
This world you see
Isn't home
It's a testing place
I am grateful with my tattered clothes
And rusty pot
So long, lost fellow!

Okay
She is now married
Everyone is blessing her
Years passed
And she isn't blessed with the fruits of the womb
Now they curse her
Calling her barren
But let me ask you
Were you the one who created what was in your womb?
Were you the one who decided when you will conceive?
Are you better than her in any way?
I'm sure her faith is stronger than yours
Because she didn't blame anyone for her inability to conceive
She rather prays harder to the Most High
Knowing every fruit comes from him.

Ask yourself
About the lives you touched with your kindness, sincerity, purity, compassion
Empathy, benevolence,

And ask yourself
About the lives you affected with your,
Pain, tears, lies

Betrayal, and deceit

You are what you impact on people.

I am a mixture of rough uneven edges
I sin
I cry
I repent
I lie
I am a long shot from perfect
And on one ever is
But every living soul is human
So it's okay.

You were gifted another day to another year
But the closure you needed to show gratitude
Was to fornicate
Because being thankful is not your thing.

I'm a deep rooted African lady
I will not bleach my skin
So I look like someone I'm not
Though many have lost their sanity
As though being lighter brings a brighter future

I don't have a flat tummy
I won't discomfort myself with a corset
My hair isn't silky or straight
I love it kinky and bouncy
My edges aren't perfect
I don't need edge control to give an illusion of what's not
My eyelashes are neither long nor full

I won't compete to look like a doll
I do have stretch marks
And I embrace them.

You see
You are poisoned to believe
That the less you cover
The more successful you become
That the more you show
The more beautiful you are
You oppress yourself in tight, heeled shoes all day long
Forgetting you are specially created
Trying hard to look like someone
Who is equally trying to look like someone else

Few have secured a stable appearance
The only genuine reflection of what you are
Is you.

Whenever I came across a bitter person
I often wondered why they choose to be bitter
When being sweet costs less
Until bitterness chose me
And my sadness refused to go away
Turning my sweetness to bitterness
Only then did I clearly understand
That people don't always choose pain
Pain chooses them
And turns to bitterness
When being brave has been stressed on
Time and again.

STEM

I am not just a woman
I was originally an outlaw for the crime of gender
This crime was never yours to validate
You were made strong
To make me stronger
You were made smart
To make me smarter
So don't douse my flames anymore
Eliminate subjugating me to the confinements of matrimony
Obliterate oppressing me with genital mutilation
Desert marginalizing me with mediocrity
Don't call me a pigeon while I am an eagle
Stop calling my strength a flicker when it's a raging tornado
Desist from calling my dreams mediocre
When they soar higher than Kilimanjaro
Stop clipping my wings
Allow me to fly
Don't push me into a kitchen and call it my calling
Don't just give me an apron and make it my identity
Stop giving me deafening silence when I need your soothing words
Quit giving me antipathy when all I demanded was empathy
Simply stop quenching my thirst for success if you cannot water them to sprout
Stop being the king of thorns when I'm always a

sunflower to you
Don't give me your thorns when I gave you my petals
Don't crumble my petals when I gave you my colors
And don't give me greyness when I gave you a rainbow
No! don't do that to me anymore

I am not just a woman
Don't just call me beautiful
Dive deeper
Calling me beautiful is nice
But calling me smart makes my heart smile
You have to wander in search of my beauty and ugliness
These eyes have brewed wordless lies in the eyes of hypocrites
My hands have countlessly cupped tears like dripping water from a tap
My mind is fierce like a scorching volcano
My spirit spins with might like a raging tornado
My ears have been battered, bruised and burnt
In the hands of mind domineering people
My tolerance button have been stumped on countlessly
Territorial abuses have been limitlessly mapped on my skin
I have journeyed through the path of heaven and hell

But I have rediscovered my strength underneath the sheets of intimidating cowardice
Because I am not just a woman
My heart, brain and soul should be heard
As much as you want yours to be
I cannot give you my understanding and receive your intentional confusion
I cannot give you listening ears while you give me hearing impaired ears
I cannot hear the society while the society mute my voice away
I simply cannot make your voice a crescendo while mine stands a chance
of an echo
I cannot give you milk and honeyed words while you give me vodka and lime
Give you silky soft hands while you give me steely grips
Embrace you with warmth while you give me a frozen body
Make your eyes merry in delight while mine bleeds a puddle of tears
Tranquilize you with wine while you distress me with opium
Mold your broken pieces with gold while you wreck my heart into shards like glass
I simply I cannot go through confinement for you and still be called a weakling
No! Don't do that to me anymore

I am not just a woman
Dive into my soul and see my yearnings
To be heard and treasured

Don't just see me as an instrument for pleasure
We are all walking tragedies at some point in life
Anybody you meet is an overflowing ocean of calm tides and raging tsunamis
But I am not a woman who hugs despair
So today I am telling the kinds of my kind
To not let the stormy days scare your dreams away
To not let the rainy days dissolve your dreams
To not let the sunny days burn your dreams away
Because there is more fire in you waiting to be reignited

So today, again
I am telling the kinds of my kind
To tell the eagle in you to not be afraid to fly
Tell the flower in you to not be afraid to bloom
Tell the thunder in you to not be afraid to strike
Tell the tsunami in you to not be afraid to rage
Tell the bee in you to not be afraid to give sweetness
Tell the butterfly in you to never cease to be beautiful inside out
Most importantly
Tell that soul in you to not be afraid to touch

hearts
Because!
We are not just women
We are Amazons
We are fighters
We are Nature's muse
We simply are not just women

We are the next generation
That will be heard, seen and celebrated
Like the icons we truly are
Because for all our lives
We have sat in a comatose state
Watching as marginalization, subjugation, and oppression
Chokehold our souls!

Well, not anymore!

I understood I was gotten from your rib
To be my protector
My shield
My muse and antidote
But you happen to be the darkness that overshadows my dreams
The lightening that scared my aspirations
The vampire that sucked out my passion
And encapsulated my worth.

Yet here I am
Pleading for support
Craving validation
Praying for acknowledgment
And seeking permission

Yet, you denied me freedom
You always told me to stay within my limits
For being a cook and a nanny is all that I'm worth
What a misogynist you are

Yet here I am
Seated,
Bundled up in despair,
Married to desolation,
depression and despondency

Only to realize I was created to be immeasurable
Interminable to supersede the four walls of your kitchen
Was that not what you dreaded,
The realization of my value?
Well I realized I am worthy
And self worth is a desideratum

And now?
I shall make history
My voice shall now be heard
I will carve out my niche in no where but the musuem

So here I am today
Pushing
Running
Flying
Touching the skies you once told me I could only stare
Climbing mountains you said I could only watch
Switching my high heeled shoes to high heeled dreams
Switching the dose of mediocrity to toast of success

Yet here I am
Expunging your suffix T in your Cant
To I can
And here I am seeing through the eyes of Oprah Winfrey, Malala Yousafzai, Ngozi Okonji owella, Mary Wollstonecraft, Ginni Rometty, Maya Angelo, Zaynab Alkali ,Queen Amina of Zazzau, Hilarry Clinton and many more other women who dared to say NO

Here I am
With my kinds ruling
Here are my kinds
As lawyers, doctors, engineers, mothers, teachers, pilots, ministers, business moguls,rulers
Soon governors or presidents even

You called this neurosis
But be rest assured it has no cure
And You dare not call my worth and right containable.

You should think twice!
Darling Misogynist

Just like the ocean you are
Mesmerize them with your beauty
But if they hurt you
Bring out the tsunami in you.

I know you're only concerned with undressing this body
But I dare you to undress this mind to naked vulnerability
Evanesce the traits of thirsty men in this soul
Ignite the fire of unconditional love in your eyes
And douse out the flames of uncertainty in mine.
Only then, shall I grant you the key to my heart and self in entirety.

Being unperturbed to slanders
Led us here
We will always wear these badges of scars
As a sign of our strength
They ought to know
We are no quitters
We are here to make forever.

He called me after several moons
He was being sarcastic to my single status
But I humbly smiled and asked him
Why his elder sister is still single
And he sheepishly told me it's all time
And I said I'm glad you acknowledge that
Never again did he mock me.

I may be smart
But I'm not smart enough to falsely utter
'I love you too'

You are unfurling with every petal
You are reaching a different phase in your life
Every unfurled petal symbolizes your growth
It's okay you are not where you want to be right now
It doesn't mean you are ill fated
You are very much blessed
Only time will unravel your blessings.

Slit me with your sword soul
Break me with your bruised heart
But this soul will spring back
I will regrow with the green blood in me.

It's okay you don't fancy boys anymore
It's okay you don't like silly jokes anymore
You don't even like games anymore
You don't fancy animation movies anymore
You don't obsess over love anymore
You are unfazed about criticisms
You are unperturbed by naysayers
But I want to tell you something
There is absolutely nothing wrong with you
But everything right with you
You are growing
And you are becoming better with age.

Never give anyone the wheel to your life
To steer at their desires
It's not submissive obedience
It's called submissive slavery.

Some people call me a snob
But I'm neither meek nor introverted
I just feel
Small talks are humorless sarcasms
And mockery to my heart.

Do not despair
For having no soulmate
Smile and remember
Its nature's law
To be created in pairs
Their hands are still on a journey
To meet yours
To love
To cherish
To embrace.

They always ask
'Doesn't it get lonely alone?
But friends are beautiful creatures'

And I answer
'Yes they are wonderful partners
But anything that does more harm than good,
Should be eradicated
And no
I would rather choose my cat
A million times, over
The friends of nowadays'

Your wrong wasn't giving pure love,
To the heart who knows not of love nor compassion
It wasn't your fault they are crooked the way they are
It simply isn't your fault they only know of lust
It's just sad you gave love
Time and time again
To people who were already married to the devil.

You loved yourself
And I loved you for that
You loved her
Because she was in love with herself
I tried to be like her
But you hated me more
Never did I know
True self-worth
Firstly lies in true self love.

I weigh more than what society calls normal
I look different
I behave different
Even an abnormal human being knows
I'm not normal
So I smile in my abnormal normal self
And toast to my abnormality.

I gave you my leaves
But you crumbled them
Now let me give you my brawny thorns
Let's see if you can touch me again.

They marginalize us as weaklings
But a normal human body
Can only withstand 45 Del (units) of pain
Thus, a woman giving birth
Feels up to 57 Del (units) of pain
So tell me
Who is the weakling here?
Because no man ever
Dared
Felt
Experienced
Such unimaginable pain in history
So just leave this argument
And take a seat
Women are more powerful than you could ever think
Defining our capabilities in a limited way
Only proves how naïve you are.

Her mind knows nothing
But the beauty of innocence
And her eyes!
Her eyes
Give you hope to turns your life around.

The moment you try to define me
In a limited way
Is the moment I will map out your ignorance
About the woman you're dealing with.

A meek person is ugly
While an ugly confident person is attractive
Vulnerability and insecurity are classless
And anything classless is uninteresting.

If they love you
They'll love you
They have no business with who you were
Your past is gone and they weren't there
This is none of their business to worry about
They should worry about the person you are today
Because this is when they are in the picture
And it matters
Inclusive of whom you hope to be in the future.

You will always be too scarred
To a man whose love is too little
But your scars will be so beautiful
To the man whose love is so truthful
How we see things is based on how we feel them.

You said I have the perfect body size
And you admired that
I lost a little
And you asked me not to lose that booty
I added a little
You told me I have too many folds
Let me trim and be perfect

But do me a favor
Control your height and be taller
Then I will control my body size
To how you want it.

Just like the nightingale you are
Never cast out the melodies in your heart.

My religion expects me to marry
It expects me to give birth
It expects me to shoulder the weight of the world
on my shoulders

The world expects me to have dry eyes
It expects me to stop dreaming
It expects me to be nothing
Other than a housewife and a mother

Well let me tell you what I expect of myself
I expect you to say
I can't
And I will
To say I wouldn't
And I will
To say I'm a weakling
And let you watch me reach mountain Everest
The more you try to define me in a limited way
Is the moment I surpass your limited
imagination
Because my mind is fierce
And I am good enough.

Stop stalking them
Stop disturbing them with calls
Stop bombarding them with mails
Stop being a pest

Start having aspirations
Start being constructively minded
Start dressing in outfits of self-respect

Dissolve this brazen marriage
Take off this hideous looking outfit of disdain you bought
And always show up in the outfit they constantly wear
Called 'HARDWORK'

There are days
I choose to paint my demons colorless
And paint my mind with butterflies.

It could be as sweet as heaven
If you make it your only home
Likewise deadly as poison
If you make it home with anyone you meet.

I made booboos
I did stupid things
I went places you wouldn't think I did
I met people you wouldn't imagine I met
I've surpassed your imagination
I'm yet to surpass an antagonist's assumption
I am a result of rough, mild, punctured, sharp, beautiful and dark edges.

To God
I'm just human
To man
I'm a mixture of unforeseeable turbulence and serenity

To myself
I am a rediscovered soul.

Be thankful
To the people who questioned your capabilities
In all honesty
They were your muse
To rediscovering your strength.

✸✿❀○❀✿✸

I see you locked at home
But when you sprightly fantasized
On how you wished you were successful
How you could have done much more with your life
And I cheerfully told you
Not to worry
I will do much more
But you looked at me with scornful eyes
And lashed out on how delusional I was
Reminding me of my gender
But you can never talk me out of my dreams
It's okay if you gave up on yours
But that alone is sad.

To allow you touch me again
Is to have my heart insulted again.

I used to sit alone
And hide in the dark
When the world gets at me
I bury my face in between my thighs
And I do what I know best
I cry!

But this time my tears declined
I tried to muster a tear
It declined
I raised my face and screamed at the dark
And my fear pushed me
        To rediscover my strength
        Strength which roared with might
        Might enough to make my fear
        nonplussed
        Nonplussed enough to run away
        Run away and never return

How did you say you feel about me again?
I want to know if your games of deceit are lit or doused
This outfit of flattery fits you fine
But not me.

You think I'm visually impaired?
But my eyes have contextually situated your '*I love yous* '
Out of the walls of my head
And tactfully placed them where they belong
Just right behind my ears.

Marijuana could be an escape
From your caged mind
But your soul, crippled at the Devils' house
Still thinks it is better caged
Than crippled.

There is a reason every human being
Has brain
Some don't have legs
Some don't have arms
But no one has no brain

There is a reason
God gave you one
It is for you to use it
By yourself
And not to keep it aside
And roam brainless

Use it!

She stood and wondered
How a statue grew a flower
But the statue asked her
How a pierced heart still beats?

There is a greater strength
In what was once broken

Pain is always a muse to a warrior.

I am no ordinary woman
Whose soul you can steal
Crack her heart into shards
Congest and cloud her mind
And make her question her worth
I am fierce

My mind is dauntless
My soul is spotless
Not an iota of self-unworthiness resides here
A woman like me is hard to be misled
By man who took self-worth as another word in the dictionary.

Some Northern parents tell you
They educated equally both genders
They tell you to try harder at school
They push you to study at your best
And you believe they truly support you
But when you come of age to aspire in life
They stunt your growth with emotional blackmail
Telling you they were submissive to their parents

When they realize your passion still radiates through your chest
They forcefully hand you an apron
And tell you that's your innate identity
Just because you are a woman
You just have to give up your dreams

Marriage is the only achievement
They say
But no
This has to stop
We could actually reach mountains no man dared to reach.

I'm sorry
I told you I'd never walk away
I'm sorry
I thought I was helping a lost, humble being
Never did I know you were bitter, lost and unapologetic
I'm sorry
I can't walk down through the path of redemption with you
But your cutting heart can never beat my luminous heart
It actually made it stronger
Giving it more reason to be distinct from yours
Thanks for making me realize how good my heart still is
In a cold world of bitterness and malice.

ROOTS

They preach how we all are one
We all came from Adam and Eve
They say they despise racism
They say they despise tribalism
But the moment you bring forth a foreigner or a southerner
Is when their Nigerian savagery comes to play
Telling you to look for your real parents
You can't bring shame to their family
And now you're trying to juggle
The meaning of what they usually say

We all are hypocrites at some point in life
We should change that!

So you mean to say
This veil of mine is a weakling on its own?
Let me tell you what this veil does
It covers mountains I carry
Marks imprinted in my soul
It's a badge of honor, a silhouette of pride
I would take forever to narrate its beauty
So go with what you know best
This veil can never be defined in a concise manner.

You might call my roots
My culture, my norms
My food, my mother tongue and everything
eccentric
But I'm proud of each and every single culture
It makes me who I am
It is my most honorable identity
So mock it and call it whatever you wish
Call the bike *'Babur'* as you wish
That Babur blood is worth
More than anything you could imagine.

You mock my religion
Calling it extreme
You mock my veil
Calling it eccentric and outdated
I wouldn't even correct your confident ignorance
If you were lettered about your religion
You would know, Mary, the mother of Jesus
Always covers up
The mother of the believers!
So who is even more of a believer between you
and I?

They tell you the man is the head of the family
And you must be submissive to him
They impart all the morals and ethics necessary in you
As they take you to your matrimonial home
But he turned out to be a beast
While they ask you to be a woman
'Don't tell anyone, the society will laugh at you'

He bruised your beautiful skin
And shattered your soul with excruciating pains
He killed the blooming lady in you
But you still stayed to be oppressed
Just because of useless societal expectations

You should also remember
Society won't be there to cry with you.

www.ingramcontent.com/pod-product-compliance
Lightning Source LLC
Chambersburg PA
CBHW051346040426
42453CB00007B/441